THE CONNECTED PARENT AND CHILD

How to Build Trust, Respect, and Attachment with Your Adopted Child

Nancy Noble

Please note the information contained within this document is for educational and entertainment purposes only. All effort has been executed to present accurate, up to date, and reliable, complete information. No warranties of any kind are declared or implied. Readers acknowledge that the author is not engaging in the rendering of legal, financial, medical or professional advice. The content within this book has been derived from various sources. Please consult a licensed professional before attempting any techniques outlined in this book. By reading this document, the reader agrees that under no circumstances is the author responsible for any losses, direct or indirect, which are incurred as a result of the use of the information contained within this document, including, but not limited to, — errors, omissions, or inaccuracies.

TABLE OF CONTENTS

I

INTRODUCTION

Raoul is playing with Sarah in the backyard. It was a game of hide and seek, with Raoul hiding in the bushes while Sarah is counting backwards from ten. I could see them from my window as I was washing the dishes. My husband Rey is reading the morning paper on the porch, looking over the kids in between sips of coffee and the headlines. I can hear Raoul squeak as Sarah catches him and they run all over the yard, laughing and having the best time of their lives. Their giggles filled the peaceful neighborhood and all seemed well. I feel very grateful at this picture perfect moment, a snapshot of a perfect family on a Sunday morning.

When you look closely at the two kids, Raoul and Sarah are the most different of siblings. Sure, even the closest of twins have their own differences, and it is quite normal to have very different characteristics among family members. Raoul is dark-haired, brown and serious, with a gaunt look on his resting face. But when you are able to make a connection with him, he can easily burst into the sunniest of smiles. His big sister Sarah is blond-haired, white and carefree, responsible but has a streak of mischief at times. They love each other very much, with Sarah always doting on her younger brother. They may look worlds apart, but they are the closest siblings I could ever hope for. With their expressive care for each other, one will never notice that they aren't really sister and brother. Not in the biological sense that is.

You see, Raoul is adopted. I've never shied away from that fact, nor have I hidden it from him or from any member of our family. When Sarah was born, Rey and I were over the moon. Sarah was a hard-earned gift, for we were trying really hard after two years of marriage. We thought one of us was barren, and then Sarah just came into the picture. She was our bundle of joy, a fulfilled promise that brought a lot of happiness to our family. After Sarah was born, I was told by the doctor that it was life-threatening for me to have another baby. Sarah would have to be it, or I could risk dying. It had something to do with my ovaries, cancer they said, and the best solution was to take the whole womb out. Sarah was a lucky gift but I was told to be grateful. In order for the ovarian cancer to be halted, I was advised to have my whole ovaries and uterus all out in one go. I was happy to have Sarah and to be granted a second life.

But I just knew I had so much more love to give. Sarah was the bright light of our family, eager and curious about the world. I was more than happy to have her around. But when I was growing up, I always imagined having a big family with at least four children. I had seven siblings and Rey came from a brood of four. We were really hoping that we could have at least four, but then the big health issue came up. We were lucky to have Sarah. But one part of me knew I wanted to have at least one more child to give my love to.

And so Rey and I talked about adopting another child. We both wanted to have a boy. It was an easy decision for all of us. Sarah was more than eager to have a younger brother. From finding an agency, to having house interviews to waiting for a match, the whole adoption process was a whirlwind of emotions. It was a mix of excitement, worry, disappointment, depression, and finally rejoicing when we found out that the agency had matched us with a young Guatemalan boy. Raoul was his name and from the moment I heard that, I loved him already. We called up the agency in Guatemala and had a chance to hear little Raoul. And I knew he was the one for us. We wanted so bad to have him around. But it took one whole year more for us to process all his immigration papers. We had to sign a lot of papers, pay a lot of fees and wait a couple of months. But it was all worth it.

Raoul completed our family. From the moment he arrived, we wanted to hug him all the time and shower him with all the love we had inside. He was a quiet kid and responded guardedly to our hugs. At first, he resisted our touches, preferring to be alone. We were quite taken aback at that because we were a very touchy family. We were told that Raoul just had to warm up to us and we should respect his process. Before long, Raoul became more familiar with our ways and was more receptive to physical touch. It was a learning curve for all of us. We had to learn and unlearn a lot of things in making Raoul part of our family. And now, Raoul and Sarah are playing in the backyard with my husband reading the morning paper. I can't wish for anything else except to be with my family.

But I knew my mission was not complete with just my family. I love Sarah, Raoul, and Rey to bits. But I felt a deeper love inside me, which wanted to reach out to other people who wanted to become parents like us. I was asked one day by the agency if I could share my experiences of adoption with a new group of curious couples. At first, I told them I didn't know what to say. But after some time of thinking, I knew I had to share Raoul's story with people and how our family evolved because of him. I accepted the invitation to speak and was so overwhelmed with the reception of the couples. They all wanted to learn more about what it meant to adopt another child, the process, the integration, etc. I wasn't exactly a speaker by training, but I love talking about Raoul. So, I gladly answered their questions.

And from one speaking engagement, I was invited to another and another. Before long, the agency was already paying me to give orientation and counseling sessions with would-be parents. I was listening to their hopes and dreams of becoming parents as I also shared my own journey. After their own adoption processes, people would come back to me and share their unique adoption experiences. I felt very proud of them as they saw how beautiful adoption was and how loving another child brought so much fulfillment. I listened to their stories of struggle, their initial fumbles at being parents, the fears and insecurities of their adopted child, and their inspiring stories of being closer as a family. I feel grateful to be given the opportunity to talk with and become friends with all these wonderful individuals and couples who have made a decision to extend their love by adopting. I guess in some way, I have helped in finding better places for these children to feel the love they deserve.

And so this book is a product of all those stories I have heard during my speaking engagements. I am proud to call these new parents my adopted friends. I wanted to capture all our struggles and triumphs as adoptive parents in this book so I could reach out to more would-be parents. I know that there are a lot of other individuals and couples who are lost but are yearning to spread their love more. May this book become your source of guidance as you begin your journey as an adoptive parent. I tell you that all the hard work is worth it. Having your own biological child is a blessing. But caring and loving for your adopted children open a different avenue of fulfillment and love we are all capable of. Let us spread this love we feel and help more children grow into families of love and care. Let us take this journey of love together.

II

THE ADOPTION PROCESS

The whole journey from having the desire to adopt to actually having your adopted child in the house involves a long process. It can be daunting and disheartening for some who thought that adoption was just like picking an item from a catalog to be delivered at your doorstep. The whole process can take as long as one month to up to a year or more. Personally, I think that it is good to have a long process of adoption. In this way, you are tested if you really want to adopt a child or just want to do it on a whim—your motivations for adopting become purified in the long process of adoption.

Each country will have its own process and laws governing adoption. My goal here is not to go to each country's specifics, but just to give you an overview. Hundreds of other websites can give you the exact details of the adoption process. This book is about developing the connection and real-life strategies of parenting an adopted child. But I think that giving you a broad overview of the process will help you decide if adoption is really for you.

First, you have to decide as a couple whether you want to adopt or not. We will dwell more on this in the next chapter, but I already want you to start thinking of that question as early as now. The decision to adopt often carries a story of struggle around it. I actually like to listen to this part when I am interviewing couples who are candidates for adoption. This is the most important part and will decide whether the couple will really pursue the long process of adoption or not.

When a decision to adopt is made, there are a number of options available. One option involves using the services of an adoption agency. These agencies will facilitate all of your documents needed for the process and help match you with the child who would best fit your home. There are several agencies in the United States, so make sure that your agency is a legitimate one and is accredited by the local government. They charge a certain fee for the facilitation process, and it would be good if you compare between agencies to feel which one you are most comfortable with.

Another option involves a private adoption. A couple may choose to adopt the child of another relative, an acquaintance, or a stranger without using an agency's services. A lawyer is called in to facilitate the process to make the adoption legal. When a legal adoption is made, the biological parents relinquish their legal rights to the child. This process is used more by couples who want greater privacy in their dealings and have enough time and resources to look for a prospective child. But this process can also be more expensive than using the agency since a lot of paper works and arrangements have to be worked out.

The last option involves international adoption. The previous two cover domestic adoptions or the adoption of children who are already American citizens or living in the United States already. In international adoption, a couple uses an agency to coordinate with an agency in a preferred country that is part of the Hague Convention on Protection of Children and Cooperation in Respect of Inter-country Adoption. Each country will have its own adoption laws and processes. There are a lot of immigration papers and processes you have to go through in order to bring the child to the United States.

Once you have decided on an option, agencies would usually conduct home visits. These are a panel of assessments made by agencies to determine who you are and your fitness to adopt. They will be asking about your own experiences of being raised up by your parents, your ideas about family, and why you want to adopt. They will conduct background checks on you, including your criminal records and financial capability. Assessors will often go to your house and check the environment where you will raise your child. From their assessment, they will decide if you are cleared for adoption or not. Your answers will also determine which child will best fit into your background.

These house visits may seem very intrusive. You might think that having the desire to adopt should be enough to get a child. But these assessments are very important not just for you but also for the child. Agencies want to make sure that the child will be in very capable parents and safe houses. They are not looking for perfect or rich parents. They are looking if you have the financial, emotional, and physical capacity to take in another human being and care for them as your own children. As much as they want children from institutions to be adopted, assessors also want to make sure that they will be sent to good homes. These children are already scarred enough from their experiences of being abandoned and institutionalized. Assessors want to make sure that these children go to families where they will be loved and cared for sustainably.

Do parents applying for adoption get rejected? Yes. Goodwill is good and laudable. But if the agency objectively finds a cause for you not to be approved for adoption, then take it as a sign that you might not be ready. Perhaps they feel that you need to create more safety features in your house or that you need to be more financially stable before you can take in another human being. Regardless, standards exist to protect both you and the child.

How much does adoption cost? The range can be as wide as adopting for free to as high as thousands of dollars. If you are using state agencies and adopting American children, then expenses are greatly reduced. If you are using private lawyers or adopting from abroad, then the costs can be very expensive. If you are quite picky in your child's characteristics, expect to pay more. I want to tell you that it costs to adopt so be prepared for it. But luckily, there are tax credits for adoption which you can avail of. Some of these tax cuts can greatly reduce your expenses to a bare minimum.

Should you adopt a newborn, an infant, a toddler, or a grown-up child? The choices are endless, but they have accompanying challenges and joys. Some people prefer babies because they want to nurture the child at a very young age. Some people prefer older kids because they can communicate their needs better. Many are not comfortable with teenagers because they seem more set in their ways. But they are still lovable, whichever stage they are. Ultimately, it is your readiness to take care of them and their particular developmental needs that will determine the choice of age group.

The emotional rollercoaster from deciding to adopt to proceeding with the adoption, or canceling it altogether, can be quite exhausting. You have to have enough emotional resources to withstand these emotional fluctuations. You can be disappointed with all the paper works and legal documents barring your child's entry into the country. You can be doubtful about your own capacity as a parent. You may feel unsure after seeing your prospective child's background. Your partner may be losing confidence. All of these issues will arise in the long process of adoption. I am telling you this not to dissuade you or to discourage you from proceeding. I am telling you this because I want you to be prepared. More than your own efforts, make sure that you have a lot of sources of emotional comfort to help you through the process. It pays to have your own family supporting you. It helps to have friends who will listen to your struggles and assure you of their presence. It is invaluable to have a partner who is willing to struggle with you to the end.

Is it worth it? Adoption is the best thing that happened to our family. It was a long process to get Raoul from Guatemala to our home. It was a journey not just in dollars and in miles but also in many emotional ups and downs. And even now, we are still riding that wave of emotions as Raoul continues to fit in our family. But I am telling you that it is worth all the trouble to adopt at the end of the day. Looking back at the adoption process, you will think that the effort is quite minimal, considering the joy an adopted child brings to the family.

III

IS ADOPTION FOR ME?

The most important question you will ever have to answer as you start this journey is the question "Why?" In the previous chapter, I have given you an overview of the whole adoption process, emphasizing that it is both long and costly. It was structured in this way to test your truest desires in going through with their process. It is better to have this question settled now than to only raise it when you struggle in the middle or towards the end of the process.

As I have mentioned in the previous chapter, I love listening to the story of why people adopt. Usually, I open my orientation to adoption talks with the question, "Why are you interested in adopting?" At first, participants are quiet, uneasily feeling if they ought to share. But when one person breaks the ice, a dam of emotional stories just floods out. I even have to cut some stories short because people are just so immersed in sharing their own stories of wanting to adopt.

Common Motivations for Adopting

The decision to adopt is not like the decision to have a dog or to buy a house. The decision is so charged with emotions that are unlike any decision. You are adopting another human being after all. And the choice to adopt is a free choice, something that is deliberately done knowing the full consequences of such an action. In my listening to too many "I want to adopt because" stories, I have classified them into particular themes worth noting. As a reader, check your own desires and see if they are also shared by others. I'm sure you will have your own unique story but it is just enriching to listen to the stories of others.

Infertile Couple

Marjorie and Bobby have been trying to have children for some years. They have been married for five years and have not produced any. There have been two miscarriages, and both have been devastating for both of them. When I asked Marjorie if they were willing to try another time, Marjorie said, "Maybe it's not for us."

It is devastating for couples to learn that they cannot have a family. In the first place, you enter into a marriage because you really want to have children. You dream of a loving partner, beautiful and obedient children, and a charming house as you walk down the aisle. But there are just some people who can't bear children.

Technology has tried to address this issue with increasing sophistication. Some couples try for in-vitro fertilization and other artificial means of producing offspring. There are some tests and supplements that are targeting the promotion of fertility in both men and women. Options for infertile couples have been increasing steadily through the years. But the technology has not reached perfection, and some couples still carry the burden of personal and social insecurity.

Couples like Marjorie and Bobby carry a great emotional burden when they finally decide to adopt. I feel especially for Marjorie and for women who can't bear children. I salute men like Bobby who stand by his wife even though one of them is infertile. I laud their love that transcends biological barriers. But society and their own families aren't as kind. Marjorie and Bobby told me during the interviews how their parents badgered them about having kids as soon as possible. When they go to reunions, the topic of reproduction always pops up, and many relatives even offer embarrassing remedies. The lack of a child even became a point of contention for the couple, a wedge trying to get in between Marjorie and Bobby. It was not appropriate to blame each other, yet they wanted to understand why their love was not enough.

But love saw them through the struggles. After the second miscarriage, Marjorie and Bobby decided that adoption was their best option. They still love each other very much and adoption was something close to what they wanted. It was ideal to have a biological child, but an adopted one filled the emptiness they both felt.

I am proud of all these couples who may have physical difficulties in reproducing and choose to adopt. They are making a good decision to continue staying together and build a family. But I want to warn you that adoption is not just a second opinion that is inferior to having a biological child. Adopting another child is a blessing in itself, which you should be grateful for. Families and society must erase the stigma that couples need a biological child to become a family. Instead of putting much stress on couples (which adds up to their incapability to reproduce), perhaps people can be more open to the possibility of adoption also as a viable first option in creating a family.

The Big Planners

I belong to this category. I have always wanted a big family, but I can only biologically produce one child because of my health condition. I also felt I had so much love inside me and I wanted to share that with another child. I just felt our family would be more complete if another child came along. And so the decision to adopt was quite easy.

But we also have to think of the consequences of this kind of adoption. How will the adoption affect the other biological children? How will the adopted child feel around the biological children? Their dynamics can be quite complicated, especially if they feel that there is a difference in how you treat them. It will be hard for parents to love children equally, and the issue of legitimacy can arise whenever you have arguments in the family. I am not saying that this will happen in all cases, but just be prepared. Adopted children should never feel that they are any less than your biological children, nor should your biological children feel that you love them less. It may take a while before they understand that you love them all, just differently.

Single Parent

Some people are determined to be single and yet want to be parents. I met June in one of the adoption orientations, and she stood out of the crowd because she was the only single among the group. I was used to having couples in our sessions, so my script was challenged upon meeting a single interested in adoption. I didn't want to put her on the spot, but I just had to ask her why she wanted to adopt. Surprisingly, she was game for the sharing.

"I am single and I choose to be single. I do not want a partner, though I have had boyfriends before. And even though I have been unfortunate in finding a partner for life, the urge to be a parent never left me. I feel that I want to love someone so deeply, but I figured I didn't need a partner for that. I knew I wanted to be a mother and I think that adopting a child can help me do just that. There is just a lot of love inside me and I want to share that with my child."

The challenges of raising a child alone are numerous to recount. The work of two people becomes a one-woman or one-man feat, with the person carrying the burden of financially, emotionally, and physically holding the family. Without a partner, it will be difficult to face the challenges of raising a family. But it is possible. I've seen single mothers raising up wonderful children all on their own. In fact, they even do a better job than if they had to rely on somebody that wasn't interested in supporting their family. And so I think it is difficult, but single individuals can adopt a child and do a fantastic job at it.

The LGBTQ Couple

There are still a lot of legal and social issues surrounding LGBTQ adoptions. But surprisingly, these people often pop up in adoption orientation sessions. In the United States, same-sex marriages are not widely accepted in several states, so the legality even of adopting a child is doubly difficult. Some people doubt their capacity to raise a child. But I, for one, support love in whichever form it takes. I think that sexual orientation should not be an issue about parenting. The responsible upbringing of children should be the main focus and not whether your parents are both men and women. But, legality is still a question, so this will be incumbent on the specific laws operating in your state.

Regardless of which motivation you fall into, it is important that you hold on to it. The thought of adopting a child can be quite intense for some and will persist for years without being acknowledged. There are some who are interested in the thought of adopting but are quite unsure of themselves. Again, I have to repeat, to be an adoptive parent does not mean that you have to be perfect. You don't have to be super-rich or come from an overly religious family to be considered a good candidate for adoption.

Adoption Precautions

But given that, I also am a strong believer that adoption is not for everyone. You may have an intense desire to adopt, but that alone is not enough to consider you a good fit for adoption. I am saying this not to discriminate against anyone, but I feel that adopted children have already gone through a lot of hurts and aches and deserve people who are capable of making them whole. So here are some considerations wherein adoption may not be the best choice for you.

Do not adopt on a whim

If you feel that adoption is a fad and you are just riding on it, better forget it. Actually, the long process of adoption really helps separate those who just like the idea of adopting and those who really want it. But understand that you are going to make a legal decision for yourself and another human being. You will be wasting a lot of resources and troubling a lot of people if you just feel like adopting on a whim. It hurts the child too, who will be expecting and waiting for you only to find out that you are dropping them when you realize it's not for you. And when you have completed the legal adoption, it will be very difficult to un-adopt the child again. So for everyone's sake, please be sure of your decision.

But there are cases when a decision from a whim translates to an actual desire to adopt. You may be joked by somebody that you look like the type to adopt. But in the process, you find yourself warming up to it. Then, that joke is a good springboard for an important decision. Just make sure that your motivation is not a joke anymore, but a real and lasting commitment to take care of another human being.

Do not adopt if you can't take care of your own self

This is actually self-explanatory. If you can't take care of yourself, how can you take care of another human being? And what does it mean to be able to take care of a human being? Many aspects have to be considered. One, you have to be financially ready to support your kid. I am not saying that you should be Bill Gates or Jeff Bezos to financially sustain a child. I am also not saying that unemployed people should not have children. I am saying that finances are very important in raising a family. If you don't have money to feed your child, buy him medicines, shelter him in a safe house, send him to school or dress him up in warm clothes, then you have to rethink your decision to adopt. Actually, the assessor will make that decision for you.

Another aspect is emotional maturity. I know it seems unfair that biological parents don't need to be emotionally mature to be considered parents. But when you are adopting, this standard is held against you. Again, I am appealing for good emotional maturity for the sake of the child. They are broken and have gone through a lot of difficulties already. If you cannot handle your own emotional swings, then there is a bigger possibility that the child may be at the losing end of that. I am not against people with mental illness. But I think before you think of adopting another human being, you should seek some help for yourself first. Adoption may not just be for you now. But in the future, when you are better, then you have more resources to be emotionally stable for another person.

Do not adopt if you feel forced to

Some couples feel that adoption is being forced on them. There may be a relative who just needs some cash and is begging you to take their kid in exchange. Or, you feel forced to adopt because your entire family is pressuring you to have children no matter how. Loving another human should be a free gift you express and bestow on another. If you feel that you are just being pressured by others, then adoption is not the solution. You may have resolved the issue now, but if you are not emotionally ready to have the kid, then both you and the kid will suffer unnecessarily. You may choose to postpone the decision only in such time that you feel that you really want to adopt on your own terms.

Don't feel forced to adopt a child just because they ask you to. This happens a lot when families visit orphanages and children tug at their sleeves, wishing to be carried. All children want to have families, but you don't need to adopt them all. Wait and pray for the right child to be matched to you because these agencies are doing their best to ensure that your child will be a good fit. If you feel strongly for one child, then mention it during interviews. This will be considered highly by the people handling your case. But trust that the process will give you the child you are meant to have.

Do not adopt if your partner is against it

Always involve your partner when making crucial decisions, such as adopting a child. Your desire to have a child might be intense. But you have to learn to communicate that desire with your partner. You are not going to raise this kid alone. You will need the love and help of your partner, so his feelings and decisions also matter. Talk about it freely between yourselves. Learn to listen to him or her and allow them to express their doubts and anxieties. Maybe they just need to vent all those feelings and thoughts out loud before they can make a decision.

Do not let the child be the reason that you break up with your partner. Children are not the wedge in relationships but the glue that keeps people together. If you feel that your partner is not yet ready to adopt, respect that and wait for the right moment. Maybe they just need some time to think for themselves. As much as you want to love another human being, you also have to learn to love your partner. Love is not about dividing between your partner and the child. Love should be about multiplying from your love from your partner to your child. The child will sense when one parent is warmer and welcoming while the other is distant. Children pick up non-verbals very easily, and they may get hurt in the process. Their feelings of being unwanted may be reinforced when one parent is really against the decision. So learn to communicate and make decisions together.

***

So think of your motivation to adopt a child and remember that constantly. It will last you through the difficult and wearisome process of adoption. When you feel like giving up, remind yourself of why you want to adopt in the first place. Remember that you have your own issues as you begin this journey. Remember that your partner also has issues that need to be respected. And together, take that journey through adoption step by step. Trust in the long process that will purify your motivations and cement your relationship as partners. These will provide the child with a good environment of a loving family.

In the next chapter, I will be discussing specific issues that may arise in caring for adopted children. These stories come from the many parents I have encountered and how I have seen them deal with it. I also come from my own experiences with Raoul and my family and the challenges we went through. I feel that when you accept that there are inherent challenges in adopting children, you will be more prepared to meet them. You are not expected to be perfect parents. But after reading these chapters, hopefully, you know a little bit more so that you can love your adopted child better.

IV

CONFRONTING FEAR

"Dylan, it's time to go to bed now," I told my adopted son on his first day in the house. He was quite bewildered with the setup, always looking suspiciously at every corner.

"Ok."

"So this is your room. Do you like your room?"

"I guess." It was hard to get things out of him but we can understand. It was his first day after all.

"If you need anything, just come over to our room." It was getting late and I thought we all had a long day. We picked Dylan up from the orphanage a couple of miles away and we were all tired. I was happy to finally bring Dylan home and my husband was ecstatic with him. But we were all tired. Tomorrow, we could catch up and start a new day as a family.

"Dylan, you can go inside now."

"Ok." I would have to get used to these one or two word replies.

I saw Dylan go inside his room. I was just watching, seeing what he would do next. From the slit of the door, I could see that he went up to his bed. But the lights were still on and the door was ajar. I think I would need to teach him a lot in the next few days.

So I went to his room and told him "Good night Dylan. I love you!"

Reluctantly, Dylan said, "I love you too."

All was well. I turned off the lights and shut the door. No sooner had I closed the door when I heard Dylan scream. I rushed inside, turned on the lights and thought something must have happened. He might have fallen out of the bed or hurt himself or something. But Dylan was just in bed screaming and crying inconsolably.

I didn't understand what was happening and I just hugged my precious boy tight. He was just clinging to me for an hour before he calmed down. Finally, he said "Mom can I keep the door open?"

"Sure, honey, if that will keep you calm."

And for many nights, I tucked Dylan in with the door wide open.

The following day, I phoned Dylan's orphanage and recounted what happened. His caretaker told me a possible reason why Dylan was so frantic. He said that when they rescued Dylan, he talked about being shut by his biological parents in a dark room when he 'behaved badly.' Dylan would scream and shout, but nobody would take him out of that dark room. And when Dylan transferred to the institution, they also committed my same error. Later, they developed the habit of just keeping the door ajar so that Dylan would not be afraid. It crushed my heart knowing what happened to Dylan. Ever since hearing that, I just wanted to hug my little Dylan. In our house now, doors of rooms are never shut in case Dylan freaks out.

This is a story from one of the participants in an adoption orientation I gave a few years back. The couple, Denis and Lucy, adopted Dylan from an orphanage from a nearby state. And this was an account of their first night. You can see from this short anecdote how adopted children see the world.

One of the deepest and hardest emotions to forget by adopted children is fear. They are afraid, whether it is as trivial as closing the door to their room or turning the lights out. Simple as these may be, these are triggers for them. Adopted children fear being abandoned and hurt because they have experienced it themselves.

We do not judge parents who give up their children for adoption. They have their own reasons for doing so. Some of them became pregnant too young and aren't able to raise them independently. Some have too many children and are too poor to feed them. Others may have all sorts of problems that cause them to abuse their own children. Whatever it is, putting up a child for adoption causes significant distress on the child's part.

A crucial part of the first days and nights of an adopted child is to address this fear. It is quite unshakeable, no matter how many times you reassure the child. Even if you tell them, "Don't be afraid," they can't help it. They will cling to this fear because their childhood experiences have created significant trauma that haunts them repeatedly. If you don't know the child's story, you can exacerbate their fear, as we have seen in the anecdote. We don't blame Lucy for shutting the door or not knowing Dylan's background. But we can see just how much Dylan is terrified at such a simple act, showing how deep his fear is. As adoptive parents, our first task is to address this fear and to assure our children that they are safe with us. How do you exactly do that? Here are some basic tips to help you make your child feels secure.

Know Their Triggers

It will always be rocky during the first days because it will be some sort of trial and error. You don't know what will set off your kid, so you just concentrate on what you usually do. When you hit a trigger, note what it is and how intense that action or word is to your child. There must be a history behind this reaction, and it is good for you to investigate that. But for now, just note all the triggers the child may have. They may be afraid of men with long beards. They may be afraid of the color grey. They may scream when they don't see you for a moment. These children will have some sort of trigger, and you have to be prepared to note that when it happens.

When you encounter the trigger, immediately stop whatever it is that is causing them to be afraid. Don't push the children to the edge just because you are curious about how they will react. You know that it makes them afraid, so immediately stop whatever it is they are afraid of. When they feel safer, maybe you can ask them why they are afraid of that particular gesture, phrase, or action. It may take time for them to tell you the story, but you will get there with patience.

Introduce Change Gradually

Lucy can't always agree with Dylan in keeping the doors open all the time. At some point, you want your child to overcome that fear. Do not rush that moment. Do not force them to get over it immediately. They are scared, and they will need some time to be assured that they are safe. When you introduce something to them, make sure that they are ready for one change at a time. They cannot process everything all at once. Do it one step at a time, so they don't get overwhelmed.

Establish Routines

In the first weeks of your child in the house, it is important to establish routines. These routines are any sort of behavior you do that is repeated over and over. If you want them to eat at a particular time, make sure that you call them at exactly the same time for days on end. If you want your child to put away his toys in an orderly manner, demonstrate to him the first time where to put his toys and then repeat it every time he plays with them. If you want them to call you a particular name, you should only use that name over and over again, "Mommy" or "Daddy." These are all important for the child to feel safe.

When one is afraid, there is an overwhelming sense of the loss of control. You don't know what is going to happen next because you are just so afraid. So to combat that, establish routines that the child will have to conform to. These routines make things predictable for the child. They know when to eat, where to put their toys, how to call you. When you do things repeatedly, the child anticipates that they will happen predictably. Because of this, they feel safer knowing what will happen. Making your child feel safe is important for building trust.

Of course, you can't always predict what will happen in the future. So when something new happens, adopted children easily panic because that is not part of their routine. They are afraid of the new because it may be dangerous for them. When something new happens to them, you can calm the child down by moving them from an unpredictable environment to an environment they can control. Go back to your routines, and that will make them feel safe. Gradually, as you introduce more new things, they will become less afraid of the new and even welcome it. But that will only come after years of routines and assurances from you.

Part of the routine is the familiarity of things and places. It might not be advisable to change too many things in the house or buy new stuff in the child's first week. They need some sort of stability as they try to ease in their new environment. They need to know that this is their bedroom, this is your bedroom, this is the living room, etc., without seeing too many drastic changes in the appearance and arrangement of things. If you are going out, limit your movement to what is essential. Show them the grocery and then come home. Go to your church and then come home. Go to the park and then come home. They should feel that their home is a place of refuge, a familiar area, a safe spot where they can always go.

V

ATTACHMENT STYLES

Psychologist Mary Ainsworth postulated a theory on attachment. Ainsworth says that at a very young age, children form a bond with their caregivers. The strength of this bond is called attachment. The quality of connectedness of children to a primary caregiver has a lasting impact on them that they carry throughout their lives. This is important for the baby because their attachment to the caregiver determines their survival.

Ainsworth devised experiments that sought to determine the effect of different attachment styles on children. The result of these experiments produced certain patterns of attachments that children may have with their primary caregivers.

Ainsworth described three main attachment patterns:

Secure Attachment

Babies who have a secure attachment with their caregivers cry when they are gone and are happy when they arrive. When the caregiver hugs them or gives them positive affirmation, the baby responds and returns it positively. When strangers are around, the child can be responsive to their affections but clearly prefers their own parents.

Parents who use this style are very responsive to the needs of their children. When the child is crying, they quickly investigate the cause and respond to it without much delay. The child then becomes secure with the constant support of the caregiver. When they grow up, these children are more secure and sensitive to other's needs. They are friendlier and are less aggressive than children who form other attachment styles.

Ambivalent Attachment

Children who form this attachment style cry when their parents leave them. When a stranger tries to calm them down, they do not respond at all and are inconsolable. When the parent returns, the child is not easily reassured. They may regard the parent with hostility, refusing to play with them, and can even be aggressive from being left out.

Parents who have caused this attachment style are often absent. When the child needs them, they are mostly away for some reason. The child cries repeatedly but receives no comfort or assurance. That is why when the parent returns and tries to give positive regard, the child is often suspicious. They think that they are going to be left again. And they respond poorly to other people outside their parents.

When they grow up, these children tend to be clingy to their family members, friends, or partners. They always think that they will be left by themselves, so they will be overly dependent on others. They find it hard to become close to other people because of this suspicion. They are afraid of separation and can be very devastated when a relationship ends.

Avoidant Attachment

Children who form this attachment style are cold to both parents and strangers. This may be because their parents have been away from them for a prolonged period. They may cry repeatedly, but nobody is there to address their needs. They simply stop crying by themselves. When the parent returns, the child does not warm up to them and remains distant, as though the parents are strangers.

When they grow up, these children are also emotionally distant from other people. They don't invest in commitments that they can be vulnerable in. They may not want to share their feelings and thoughts with anybody else because they want to project an image of strength.

Disorganized Attachment

The fourth attachment style was formulated by psychologists Main and Solomon. These researchers added the last style to Ainsworth's existing attachment styles after noticing that some children did not fit the three previous patterns.

Children who develop this attachment style don't actually have a consistent attachment to caregivers and strangers. These children may have several caregivers in their life, such as parents or nannies that change every year, or relatives who took them in for a short time. The lack of consistency in caregivers makes the child confused and dazed with all the changes. They cannot form a consistent and secure relationship with any caregiver. They don't know if they will be happy with the return of a parent who might leave them. They don't know if they will cry when their parents leave because another caregiver may provide their needs.

When they grow up, these children also exhibit extremes in behavior. They can be avoidant to some people and rebellious to some. They may act like old people to their peers because caregivers' differences made them exposed to different caregiving styles. But they have no clear patterns in relating with people.

These are not hard and fast rules but simply psychologists' theories on possible explanations of how our connectedness to our parents or caregivers affects children and how they will grow up as adults. They are in no way predicting that your child will really become aloof as an adult if the child did not receive any care at all. We are still unique individuals but are influenced by our past experiences.

***

Where do you come in these attachment theories? You are not the primary caregiver because the biological parent served that purpose. Even for a short time from birth leading to the adoption, the connection of the biological mother and the child will influence the child. In that sense, they are already prone to some ambivalent, avoidant, or disorganized attachment style. But what is hopeful is that as adoptive parents, you have the responsibility and the unique opportunity to correct an established attachment style to one that is more secure. You may not be able to undo the damage of being separated from the biological caregiver, but you can be a good primary caregiver that the child can be securely attached to. All you need is to be consistent and reliable in addressing their needs and giving unconditional love.

VI

COMMUNICATING NEEDS

I noticed Tranh's peculiar behavior right on our first meal. We had brought her home from an institution in Vietnam, and we decided to feed her her familiar food. I didn't know any Vietnamese dishes, but I managed to research some simple ones over the Internet. I wanted Tranh to have a good impression, and so I made a lot of food.

We settled down for lunch and prayed before meals. I can see that Tranh was just overwhelmed with the huge bounty of food in front of her. I got her a serving of rice, some meat, a lot of vegetables and a bowl of soup. She looked at me inquiringly, as though asking for permission to eat.

"Go ahead honey. Eat as much as you want."

To my surprise, that small, shy girl began to gobble up the food quite quickly. The plate was full when I gave it to her. But in less than five minutes, she was able to consume everything, and the plate and bowl were gleaming empty. I don't know what they were feeding her back then, but she must be so hungry. I helped her for a second and a third before Tranh finally told us she was full. I love seeing her eat. I'm not the best cook out there, but the way Tranh finished the food, she must have loved my cooking.

And so it was like that for every meal. Tranh would eat large amounts of food at a very quick pace. We kept telling her to chew her food properly and that there wouldn't be a shortage of food any time soon. But she just kept on gobbling the food the way she was used to. And I thought that was just alright.

But after several weeks, I noticed a strange behavior in my adopted daughter. I have this cookie jar, which I always keep in stock because I really like chocolate cookies. On grocery day, I would buy a pack of cookies and fill the jar to the brim. And usually, the cookie jar would last us for a week. I kept it in my room because I wanted it to be within reach whenever I work from home.

One day, I was surprised that the cookie jar was already half empty just after a day of groceries. I jokingly accused my husband Nick of stealing the cookies just to tease me, but he vehemently denied it. Maybe I wasn't conscious of how much cookie I was eating, so I thought it was just me. I resolved to let the matter slide.

But the following day, the entire jar was empty. I don't think Nick would prank me with this feat because he was not the type. I knew I didn't eat any cookies the whole day. And so a sneaky thought came up to me that perhaps Tranh had something to do with it. And literally, I just followed the cookie trail right to her room. I noticed the crumbs of chocolate cookies all the way to her room.

I went up to Tranh, who was in her bedroom playing with a doll we gave her. I asked her if she got any of the cookies in the room, and she just said, "I don't know."

"What do you mean you don't know, honey? Did you eat the cookies?"

There was a long pause, and then she just burst out crying. I didn't understand what was happening. It was just the cookies for me, and perhaps I was too strong on Tranh. I hugged her tightly, wishing to hug away all her fears. She just kept on crying and holding on to me tight.

When she calmed down after a while, I asked her again, "Tranh did you eat the cookies?"

"No." I was kind of surprised at that. What was she crying for?

"So where are the cookies?"

Tranh reluctantly looked at me and then went on all fours. She reached out under the bed and pulled out the pile of cookies underneath. She had been keeping them all along under her bed, uneaten but piled neatly.

One of the most common behaviors seen in adopted children is hoarding. They tend to accumulate goods like food, toys, crayons, money, clothes, and all sorts of stuff just for the sake of accumulating them. Rebeca noticed this behavior in her adopted daughter quite early, and she sought counsel from me. I thought that Tranh's behavior was a classic example of this hoarding behavior.

Why do they hoard? As we have seen in the previous chapter, behaviors are reinforced as a product of their past experiences. I am not discriminating against the work of orphanages and other institutions handling children here and abroad. I believe that they are doing an important job and that their efforts are laudable. But that being said, in some countries, resources are just so hard up that some institutions are defunded. It is deplorable that some states do not give adequate funding and resources for the care of children. These institutions have to make do with whatever they have. Try as they may to feed all the children, caretakers often have to budget the meal to cater to everyone. There are a lot of abandoned children, and the resources are just very scarce.

During meal times, children in some institutions have to eat their food fast; otherwise, it may be taken away from them by other kids. They are just so hungry and protective of the little food they have. They are always worried that they may not have enough food for the next meal, and so they gobble what is available before it disappears.

When visitors come and feed the kids, they are always very eager and excited. Usually, donors would give candies or food packages, especially during Christmas or the holidays. But caretakers would often get the gifts and store them first to distribute them equally among the children. As a reaction, the children would often store the gifts given to them in places where the caretakers cannot reach them. It becomes some sort of treasure box. It's quite sad that this happens, and they can carry this hoarding behavior to adulthood.

Even with the assurance of food in their new house, adopted children carry that stigma and will find ways to keep a stash of food or goodies just for themselves. It may be a sign that they are still wary of trusting you, but it may also just be a carryover of their past behavior. Even if you tell them that there is enough food, they will still gobble up meals quickly. It may be a surprising feat you don't usually see during lunchtimes, so be prepared when it happens.

You can allow this behavior for a few weeks because they are still adjusting. But you can't let this continue for a very long time. From hoarding food, the behavior can carry over to other items such as toys, school supplies, or clothing items. But they can also graduate from this and may even resort to stealing more valuable items. Plus, the hoarding behavior tends to accumulate a lot of unused items in an area. You may have a mix of garbage, rotting food, broken toys, or dirty laundry all piled up in one area. The hoarding behavior is all about accumulating more and more items. Hoarders also don't want to throw anything away because it may be useful to them at some time they don't know. The compulsion to accumulate may affect your child's behavior if you don't address the underlying issue.

In my encounter with parents of hoarders, I have found out that a mix of teaching good communication skills, constant reassurance, and a lot of discipline is necessary for the behavior to be adequately addressed. Parents usually have a hard time dealing with hoarders, and they simply end up giving in to the binging behavior. This failure to teach can result in reinforcing the behavior further. And, when you give in to their fast-eating habits, their nutrition can be compromised. They either don't absorb all the nutrients they ingest, or they end up obese.

This is just one example out of many other issues children may carry. Here are the strategies on how to communicate with your child and address his needs. Please note that these also may apply to other behavioral issues.

Learning To Speak

One of the key elements in addressing any behavioral problem is communication. You have to teach your child how to communicate their needs in a timely and appropriate way. Language skills are important to develop. Children have different rates of maturing in this aspect. Several factors are needed to be considered when you are teaching your child how to properly communicate their needs.

Age

Of course, younger children will have simpler language skills than older children. Intelligence is cumulative, and so you cannot expect very young children to immediately start talking about what they want if they cannot even form simple words. So you have to determine the expressive and receptive language capability of your child.

But note that you also have to observe if there are language delays. If you feel that your child is not speaking in full sentences by age 3 or 4, or that they tend to point to items rather than say the name aloud, you might want to consult a developmental pediatrician for this. There are a lot of developmental abnormalities that can develop, which manifest as language difficulty. You have to spot this early on because your child will have difficulty in school when these are not addressed. The sooner you spot the problem, the faster they can be helped.

Race

It is an obvious consideration if you are adopting a child from another culture. They may have been raised in their own language, and that can get stuck for a while. These language barriers may prevent you from effectively communicating with them, and you may be forced to resort to sign or body language to communicate. There may be certain expressions or customs that are particular to each of your cultures, and you have to be careful lest you say something bad or awkward in their language. It pays to learn their culture as much as you want them to learn yours.

What is good with children is that they are still developing their language skills. They can adapt to languages easily as long as they are constantly exposed to them. They can have a mother language or the language that they were first taught, and they can have a functional language, the language that they use in everyday life. Whatever language you are using in the house, it is best to stick with it and allow the child to hear it over and over again. Gradually, they will adopt the language easily.

Engagement

Children who are not talked to will not be able to develop their language skills. Children who are not free to express themselves will lose whatever language skill they have. This may seem very obvious, but it is often taken for granted in some households. In some institutions, for example, there are just so many children and so few caretakers. Therefore the attention to each child is uneven. There may be favorites in the bunch who get to hog up all the attention even of visitors. And then some children are not always spoken to. When this happens, there is less stimulus in their brain, and hence, parts responsible for language will not develop maturely. If they are exposed to unkind words in an abusive household where they came from, they may also resort to silence as a coping mechanism. Words may be very traumatic for them as they have been used to hurt them or other family members. They can even imbibe the cursing that they see from their biological parents. The violence may be so normal that they don't know it isn't until they use it on you. It may be good for you to do a background check on your child before taking them in just to have a clearer picture of what you are getting into.

***

You are not required to talk to them all the time. Of course, you still have your own life. You just need to provide them with enough stimulus to be exposed to polite and friendly language. Some parents are just too busy with their work. When they go home, they are too tired to engage in any conversation. But if you are taking care of any child, biological or adopted, they need your time and effort to help them grow in their language and social skills. As they listen to you, show them that you are also interested in their stories, no matter how trivial it may be. Adopted children are quite observant, and if they feel that they are not wanted, they will keep quiet. When that happens, perhaps you need to be more sensitive and probe into their silence. They will not volunteer their thoughts and feelings to you, so you have to invite them to share it out. Mutual respect is shared when two people know how to listen to each other. Children can easily sense that and will remember it until adulthood.

Given these considerations of age, race, and level of engagement, you will now have to teach them how to express their needs verbally. The main problem in dealing with hoarding is that there is a need inside them that wants to be expressed but is not verbalized correctly. In their frustration to communicate, children often use physical means such as pointing to the desired object instead of talking and even taking the object without permission. To teach your kids how to express their desire, you can follow the format of FEEL-WANT-DO.

Feel

The first thing you ask the child is not to ask what they want, but how they feel. This is an important insight you should commit to memory. If you simply jump to the object of desire, then the conversation is finished, without the child learning to express anything. But the desire underlies a deeper emotion that the child must learn to recognize. If they remain fixated on the object that they want, they will not be able to realize what is triggering them to desire that object in the first place. Emotions are the primal stimuli in children, and they have to learn how to name what they are feeling.

To illustrate this point, let us take a child's request for a piece of cake. So you ask your child what they want, and he answers you, "I want cake." You can go ahead and give the cake to the child, and the story is finished. But they might ask again and again for a cake, and if you don't investigate the cause of this request, you are simply going to give them cake repeatedly. But if you ask them, "What are you feeling?" then it will make them think about their own motivation for wanting that object. Suppose you say, "Are you hungry? That's why you want cake?" and you get an answer of "No," then you will think twice about giving the cake. The child is not hungry and yet wants the cake. The feeling does not match the object of desire. Perhaps the child is anxious and needs the cake to feel safe or assured that there is food. But they have to name that feeling of anxiety and not just let it grip them with impulsive grabbing.

There are four basic feelings we can have: sad, mad, glad, and afraid. Within these emotions is a constellation of similar feelings with varying degrees. For example, the family group of sadness can range from boredom to dissatisfaction, from loneliness to longing, from sadness to devastation, from desolation to depression. Children have to use the exact word that matches their feelings so they can be clear. As adults, this is already very difficult for us, but we should start teaching kids about naming feelings, forming that habit early on. When they cannot verbalize what they are feeling, they will resort to physical expressions that may not be clear or may even pose a danger to themselves and others. Children should be empowered and taught how to use words to express what they feel.

Want

From asking about feelings, you have to ask them what they want. Emphasize here that children need to be specific about what they want. They cannot just point to a corner of the house and expect you to know what they are pointing to. They may not have words yet to name everything, and so you have to widen their vocabulary and teach them the proper name of things. Instead of going around the house and telling the kid, "Is this what you like? Is this the one?" make them tell you exactly what it is that they want. The more specific they are with naming their desire, the more they can develop their expression skills. If you feel that the child is not specific enough, then ask him for more details so that they learn to describe, as well as name.

Do

After naming what they want, ask your child what they want you to do. It is not enough that they want something. They have to tell you exactly what to do. If they want a cookie, then they should ask if you could get them one. If they want to play, they should ask your permission. If they want to watch television, then they should tell you to pass the remote. The desire must be accompanied by a specific request or course of action. So what if you know what they want? Some parents will automatically give the object desired. But there is greater learning involved when the child is allowed to verbalize what exactly they want to happen. Maybe they want you to give it to them. Or maybe, they want to do it for themselves. When you give them that opportunity to act, you are empowering them instead of making them dependent on you. There are a range of actions that are open to you and the child after the object of desire has been named. They can even choose not to act on their desires and simply tell you that "It's a nice toy" or "It's a pretty dress" without really asking that it be given to them. The child must realize that there are so many other possibilities aside from acting on their impulse. This will help them develop their executive skills or functions to integrate different signals in the brain. When a child is able to think of possible courses of action, their perspective is widened.

So apply the FEEL-WANT-DO format when you address your child. They must identify exactly what they feel, exactly what they want, and exactly what they want done. It will take some time, even for you, to get used to this way of expressing needs. But when you practice this format a lot, then the child will learn new words and become more specific in expressing his needs. The communication gap is reduced when you empower your kid to be specific in words.

Please and thank you = I love you

Part of showing your love for your child is teaching them how to say please and thank you. These are one of the first few words you should teach them because it opens a respectful way of communicating. Children who are taught to say "please" and "thank you" do not just mouth out words of courtesy and politeness. They imbibe the values attributed to saying these words. These are not just words said routinely to please people. These are words that express your love for the person you are saying that to.

When you say "Please" to a person, what are you really teaching the child? Saying "please" means you respect the other person. You value their love, and so you don't grab things right away but wait for them to give it to you. When you teach the child to say "Please," it is a way of acknowledging their need for you as well as their readiness to wait if you will grant their request or not. "Please give me my toy" is very different from "Give me my toy." The latter is a command, an aggressive and offending expression of a want. It sidesteps your authority as an adult when you are commanded by your child. But when 'please' is said before the request, there is that recognition of love and respect, a tentative plea for you to grant their desire.

Saying "thank you" instills the value of gratitude in children. More than focusing on the item given, "thank you" emphasizes the relationship between the giver and the receiver. The giver loves the receiver, and the receiver acknowledges that love by saying "thank you." Being a gift, the item comes from the generosity of the giver. When a child learns to say "thank you," he acknowledges the goodness of the person giving. It is not because the child deserves that toy so that he can demand it from his parents. "Thank you" acknowledges that the child is the recipient of the goodness and love of his parents.

So, make it a habit in your house to say "Please" and "thank you." As adults, we should use it more often in the house and not just with children but with everyone else. It is not about power dynamics or an issue of being indebted to anyone. When we say "please" or "thank you," we are simply saying that we love and respect that person, regardless of age. And when the child sees you using these words, then they are going to use it as frequently too.

Saying "No"

One of the most traumatic words adopted children will hear is "No." They have experienced a lot of rejections already in their previous homes. They heard it from visitors in the institution who can only stay for an hour or two. When children request for a longer time to be hugged or caressed, the deadlines and schedules of visitors seem to tell them "No." And, of course, the biggest "No" they ever heard and felt came from their immediate biological parents. We can understand that the parent may be undergoing something or might not be ready yet to handle a child. But the child does not understand this. To them, being abandoned by their parents is a big "No."

And so, when you begin teaching the valuable lesson of "No," know that there is a trauma in every adopted child when they hear that word. They will equate that word to being rejected and not being loved. They will feel less secure and sure of themselves and your love for them. They may feel loved and cared for in your home as they stay longer in your house. But when they encounter a "No," all the bad memories of their past can come flooding in, wiping away your good efforts.

And yet, you should teach them how to accept a "No." You must be able to find a way to make your adopted child feel that a "No" is not always a rejection of their person, but another way of saying "I love you." This might be difficult to grasp for children, but this also applies to adults. But it is necessary to say "No" when we want to protect our children from the harm they cannot see. For example, your child might ask you for more cookies. But if you give them every time they ask for it, you are not feeding them nutritious food. You are reinforcing their manipulative character by always giving in to their wishes. But as an adult, you can see that saying "No" to their requests is good for them, for their health and well-being. The problem really lies in how you communicate that "No" as another expression of "I love you."

One way to say "No" to your child's request is to explain the reason behind your decision. You might think that you don't need to because it's self-explanatory. But in truth, children don't understand why things happen. They will only react to things, and the "No" from you may be interpreted as an outright rejection. You still need to explain to your child why you are refusing their requests now. In very simple terms, they need to understand that you are taking their best interests when you say "No." For example, you can explain to your child that you are not giving them cookies anymore because they need to eat more of their vegetables and fruits. You can tell them that they already ate one cookie, and they can get another tomorrow. Or you can tell them that their siblings might want a cookie, and you can invite them to share that with others. You can tell them that eating too many cookies can ruin their teeth, or cause them to lose appetite during meal times, or make them feel sluggish during the day. Explain your decision in terms that children can readily understand. Don't cop out and say, "They should know that" because they really don't. It is our responsibility to make rational choices and not just act arbitrarily.

It does not help when you say "No, because I said so" because the reference is more to your power as an adult and the parent rather than the decision's rationality. "I said so" does not invite a conversation but shuts the door to any communication. You may have gotten your way, but you have also created barriers between you and the child. When the child can see that the decision is actually rational and makes sense, they are going to understand that "No" means "I love you."

Another way you can phrase the word "No" is to use temporal terms. This "No" can be a refusal of the request at this time but does not mean that it cannot be granted at another time. In this form of "No," you are teaching the child two things: the appropriateness of actions and the value of waiting. You have to tell your child that there is a proper time for everything. If they want to play outside at night, it is considered inappropriate because they may not see what they are doing. They can play tomorrow during the day when they feel more rested. When children can see how actions have proper timing, they will accept social norms acceptable to others. When you say "No, not today," you are opening the possibility that tomorrow or another time is ok to proceed with their request. It teaches the kid to wait, and that can be anxiety-filling but also maturing for the child. They have to wait for their turn in the slide, wait for meal times to eat, and wait to be given a treat inside of grabbing from the cookie jar. When children are made to wait, they are given time to weigh their decisions. They can reflect more on their feelings and make better decisions because they have waited long enough. In this way, the "No" is not very traumatic at all but actually challenging and brain-forming.

Saying "Enough"

The last word I want you to teach your child is the word 'enough.' When do we say that it is enough? Children need to learn this lesson to become aware of limits. I think that children who are not taught what 'enough' means carry that mindset in adulthood. There is much greed and selfishness in the world today because people don't know the meaning of enough. Everybody is just obsessed with getting more money, more power, more cars, more houses, more investments, more time, and more resources. And when adults subscribe to this, we can only predict that the children will imbibe this mentality.

Teaching 'enough' has many levels. You have to teach your child the value of having 'enough' using terms they can understand. It is difficult to teach what 'enough' means because it is a relative term, not an objective measurement across all indices. But you can still explain what 'enough' means to children. I like demonstrating 'enough' using cookies. Let me illustrate.

I explain to my child that 'enough' is like an imaginary line between 'good' and 'not so good,' or 'happy' and 'not so happy.' I give my child a cookie, and I ask him, "Is it good or not so good?" And he'd tell me, "It's good." And I'd give him another cookie and ask him the same question, "Is it good or not so good?" He would always tell me that the cookies tasted so good. I will do the same act over and over again. Usually, I hit a point at five cookies. After the fifth, I'd ask my child, "Is it good or not so good?" and by that time, he would really feel very full and would say, "I don't like it anymore." And that is when I tell him that he has had enough. When you say that something is enough, you are telling the kid the range of possibilities between what is good for him and what will hurt him if he gets more of it. I explain that if they eat too many cookies, then they are going to have a tummy ache. If they eat cookies every day, their teeth may be filled with cavities, or that they may grow too fat to fit into their clothes. That usually gets my child, and he understands that 'enough' is something that you can feel physically.

I extend this teaching to other things aside from food. I tell my child, watching television for an hour is good and enjoyable. But if I make him watch television for 24 hours, then it is not good for him. Therefore, we must set limits so that watching television is still enjoyable. I remind him that anything in excess of what is enough is already harmful to your body and mind.

I also teach 'enough' not just in reference to the child's physical and mental well-being. I want my children to have a sense of compassion and concern for others. Again, I use the cookie method for this. I tell Raoul to count all the cookies in a jar. Raoul likes to display his counting skills, so I applaud him as he announces 'twenty' with accuracy. I then ask him, "So how many can you eat?" And confidently, he will respond, "I can eat all twenty." Ok, I take that.

But then I would pose to him another question. "How many are in the house?" Raoul will take his time and arrive at "Four. Mommy, Daddy, Sarah, and me." I proceed with this line of questioning. "Do you think that Mommy, Daddy, and Sarah" would also like some cookies?

Raoul may have an idea where this was heading and so he reluctantly says, "Yes, I guess so."

"So if you eat all twenty cookies, then how many are left for Mommy, Daddy, and Sarah to eat?"

Raoul gets the idea at this point. "None. Yeah, maybe I can just share."

When I hear this, my ears are clapping with joy. My son finally knows how to think of other people aside from himself. This is a milestone for children to realize that they have to go beyond their ego and selfish concerns. When they realize that there are other people who like what they want, they will think twice about hoarding. They will begin to think of the consequences of their action and how it can affect others. Sure, they may not be as generous at first. But when you probe them most of the time with these questions, they are going to get an idea of what it means 'to have enough for me' and 'to have enough to share.' You will see that children actually like sharing things because it multiplies the joy that they feel.

Again, set the example for your children. In your own lifestyle, do you practice living only with enough needs and wants? When children see that you are generous and make others happy when you share, then they will also feel more inclined to share what they have. But when they see that you are also buying and buying stuff that you don't need, then they will copy what they are exposed to. Be the example of 'having enough to share' to your children.

VII

BUILDING CONFIDENCE

Christian came home from school and went straight to his room. I was preparing dinner when he arrived, and I expected him to drop by the kitchen as he usually did. Our afternoon routine was that he would come to the kitchen and help me out with peeling vegetables or washing plates. And he would tell me all sorts of stories about his day in school, from the questions his teacher asked to his sharing lunches with Jeremy and Nathan. He was almost unstoppable in his narration. And I love that part. He used to be very shy when we first arrived at home. We were matched with him through an agency. He was everything we dreamt of. But he was extremely shy and took a long time before he could even speak full sentences. It took him some time to warm up, but now, he could talk about everything.

But today was different. It was a different Christian who arrived because it wasn't like him to just go straight to his room. I figured that something was up, but I allowed him to have his moment. I figured out he would tell me in his own time. And so I waited until dinner time. My husband arrived and we were all settled at the table. After saying grace and passing the portions, I casually asked:

"Is there something bothering you Christian? Do you want to tell us anything?"

"No. it's ok. I'm just tired I think."

"Did something happen in school? Do you want to tell us about it?"

"Nothing mom."

"Ok if you say so. Just remember you can talk to us anytime, honey."

And dinner proceeded in odd silence. I exchanged glances with my husband and told him with my eyes to quit probing. Later on, we talked about what happened and we decided we wouldn't push Christian to tell us until he was ready.

The whole week, it was like that. Christian would come in and go straight to his room. He would still kiss me, but I knew there was something wrong. He usually tells me everything, but now, he is acting too secretive for my liking.

One day, I just couldn't stand his odd behavior and I cornered him as he arrived from school. I went up to his room and said:

"Christian this has got to stop. Tell me what's happening? Why are you looking so glum and quiet?"

"Stop asking Mom. I don't want to talk about it!" It was the first time I heard him raise his voice. I wasn't going to take this lightly.

"Don't take that tone with me young man. I'm your mother and you have to tell me what's going on. Did somebody hurt you? Is anybody in your class bullying you?"

"No mom, just leave me alone! I don't need your help."

I was quite taken aback by that outburst but I let it slip. Was my son going through something that should concern me? Or was this natural teenage angst? I better find out.

And so if my son would not let me in on his secret, a dutiful mother has her own ways of still knowing. The following day, I went to Christian's teacher and asked if there was any issue with my son. I was expecting something like a case of bullying or some prank played on my child. But the teacher told me one very minor detail.

"Well, Mrs. Thompson, Christian is doing well in school. He has many friends, and I don't think anybody is bullying him. It's just that there is this quiz in Mathematics that he got one of the lowest scores. He passed alright, but it wasn't his usual score. But he was able to do well in the succeeding tests. Maybe he just had difficulty in that particular lesson. But I did notice that he took that quiz quite badly. I tried assuring him it was alright, but he just felt so down. Maybe he could do with a little more cheering up at home."

Well, so much for my fears. My child had a low score in one test and he felt that it was the end of the world. That night, I just hugged my little Christian tight and said,

"You are smart and I love you very much Christian, more than any test on earth."

Christian looked at me quizzically and said, "So you know."

"Sure honey, and it's alright. You can tell me everything and I won't love you less. Just promise me that you will be more open with us."

"Ok Mom, thank you."

Every person at some point in their lives will encounter some sort of failure or rejection. It is a part of life, a human experience we all have to go through. We have our own big and small failures. And no matter how much we try to be good at what we do, we will still continue making errors. These mistakes show us how vulnerable we are, how limited we can be, and where we can improve on. We will continue to experience forms of failure and rejection as we strive to be our best selves.

Of course, it is hard to accept these failures. The irony is that nobody wants to fail, and yet failure is part of our life. We form our own coping mechanisms to deal with the failure. Some try to shrug it off by diverting their attention to something else. Some eat to vent out their frustration. Some people just need to talk to friends or family members, and they will feel alright. We all need some reassurance that we are still good people in spite of objective mistakes.

But some people take failures harder than most. They brood about it for days, preferring to stay holed up inside their rooms and staying away from friends. Some are even pushed to the brink of depression and anxiety. We have different coping mechanisms with failure, but some just take it more personally that it really affects other aspects of their lives. And this is where they need the most help from other people.

Adopted children commit mistakes just like everybody else. They will encounter difficulties in school, arguments with their friends, misunderstandings with family members, frustrations with their own selves. And they will form their own coping mechanisms. Some will come out stronger after these mistakes as they try to bounce back. But some will cope with failure poorly. Adopted children are more prone to depression and anxiety than other children. This may be due to the traumatic experiences they've had compared to other children.

Again, we will need to dig some more into their past before they arrive in your home. You may uncover that perhaps in the institution where they were fostered, they had experiences where they were disciplined and took it badly. Perhaps they came from families where they were physically and verbally abused. And the very fact that they were set for adoption can mean to them as the ultimate proof of rejection. They may feel unwanted, inadequate, stupid, and even unlovable.

They may keep all the negativity and insecurity for the rest of their lives. And even when they are already in good homes or have good careers as adults, they may still carry that trauma. They have difficulty coping with present tensions and stressors because they are not able to resolve past issues. They may have trouble concentrating in school because they feel so pressured to perform for you. They love you very much as adoptive parents, and so they feel pressured to be perfect so as to not lose that sense of security and love. They are harder on themselves, aspiring for perfection because they are afraid they will lose you and everything that matters to them now. Your very kindness and warmth may make them feel guilty that they are not doing well.

Usually, there is a trigger event that sets off the child. It can be a low grade in school or a fight with a friend. It could be a disciplinary action you made or a taunt from a stranger they overheard. It could be as random as hearing about orphanages on television or a dish that reminds them of their previous home. The triggers are endless and unique to the child experiencing that trauma. But from that incident, they will launch to a spiral of self-protective measures.

Common Depressive and Anxious Behavior in Children

What particular behaviors will alert you that your child may be depressed or anxious about something? What is good with younger children is that they are very transparent with their emotions. If they feel sad, you know that they are sad through their face, mood, and general dislike for activities. If they feel happy, you will know that they are giddy and willing to play. But with older children, the signs are not too obvious. They are beginning to be like adults who are difficult to read. You really have to know your child and their particular expressions of emotions so that you can have a more personalized understanding of their internal state. But here are some common behavioral indications that your child may be undergoing something:

Changes in Behavior

If your child is normally talkative and bubbly, and then begins to be more quiet and introverted, you might want to inquire if there is something you need to talk about. But the reverse can also be true. If a quiet and reserved child suddenly becomes too talkative and frantic, you still have to investigate where the shift in energy is coming from. Being too busy may be a coping mechanism.

Avoiding Social Interaction

If your child spends more of his time in the room and refuses to play with friends, you have to investigate. There are some children who are more introverted than others but will play with you and with people they are comfortable with.

Children are naturally sociable, so spending too much time in the room may be a red flag.

Change in Sleeping or Eating Habits

These activities are rather easy to observe and may give you a clue. When a child is in either extreme, which is not their usual activity, then it may be cause for concern. They may suddenly feel like sleeping the whole day or they may want to keep on playing and writing all night long which is not their usual. Children may suddenly want to eat more and more food or they may refuse to eat at all. These swings in behavior may be some form of coping mechanism. They feel inadequate and so they will fill that emptiness with something, either with food or sleep.

General Sad Mood

You know your child when they are sad. Check this if regularly pleasurable activities suddenly make them feel dissatisfied or even uninterested. They may like playing with their toy dolls. But when you see them play, they feel forced or bored. They may like going out to the park. But now, you see that they are less happy when they stroll on the grounds. Something is bothering them, and it may be good to have a little chat.

***

How can we help our children help themselves? Ultimately, they should be the ones who must make that realization that they are lovable and good persons. No matter how much we reassure them, they have to realize that on their own. And this can take a lot of time for them. Trauma is especially difficult to address, and they may need some form of professional help. But on your own, you can provide some form of comfort to them in times when they feel like a total failure. Here are some examples of constructive interventions you can provide to your children who are undergoing feelings of rejection and failure.

Assurance

What Christian's mother did when she found out about his failure is a good example of positive reassurance. She was able to communicate that in two ways: verbal and non-verbal. Children dealing with insecurity are always seeking validation from their caregivers. They may not express it well, but they want to know if they are doing well, if they are good people, if they are lovable. Their efforts to be good at school, to be friendly with peers, to help out in the house may all be meant for them to earn your love. They love you so much that they are afraid that small mistakes might compromise your love for them.

Find ways then of reassuring them of your love and support. You can show it in words by praising their efforts or the outstanding work that they do.

They will feel good knowing that you observe the little things they do for you. Just be mindful that you are genuine in your praise and not forcing the issue. For example, they already failed in Math, and yet you call them Math genius. More than being reassuring, it will come across as sarcastic or adding salt to the injury. Just express your assurance sincerely without being overly patronizing.

Reassurance can also come in the form of physical presence and touch. When you are there for them in their vulnerable moments, they will feel assured that you still support them. Hugging can be a powerful message to them that you are there for them no matter what. This may be tiring for you but make an effort especially in the times that they feel so down. Gradually, they will be able to bounce back from the failure and will need less of your assurance when they know you are always there to give it to them.

In some cases, you can treat your child out just to make them feel better. Going out for ice cream can be a good treat just to get those happy hormones kicking. It is not meant to solve their problem but it can help brighten their mood. These tangible treats can uplift their spirit even for just a while.

Distinguish Between Person and Act

When talking to children about failure, I recommend using the approach of FEEL-THINK-DO. Just like in the previous chapters, you have to start with asking first how the child feels about the failure. This might seem trivial because you can already see that they are sad or disappointed. But it pays to hear it from the child himself. They have to acknowledge that they are having a particular feeling and that they can specify what it is. We have previously emphasized that being specific with the feeling and its particular intensity will help the child understand what they are going through.

In the thinking part, you have to guide the children to understand the difference between 'person' and 'act'. When I talk to Raoul about this, I tell him that I love him no matter what. So the 'person' doing the action is lovable beyond anything they do. Even if he fails, I will always love him because he is my son. Nothing can change that, not even if he fails in a quiz or breaks his toy.

Now, we have to focus on what exactly happened, the incident. That constitutes the 'act' part. So when he tells me, for example, that his friends did not share their lunches with him the day before, we can discuss that particular act. I love Raoul for who he is as a person. But we also need to distinguish that person from the act that happened. I would probe further and try to make Raoul think of possible reasons why that happened. I can ask him if this happens all of the time or just this particular afternoon. I can make him think of other friends who are willing to share lunches with him. I can ask if perhaps they didn't like his particular food or that they weren't in the mood. When you dissect an issue, you have to make the child think of other possibilities instead of his fixed thinking that he is unlikeable or unworthy of being loved. When the child begins to realize that there are a lot of other explanations aside from his own that also makes sense, then they begin to be more mature in their thinking.

This can also work for other issues. If you feel that your child committed something wrong and you want to discipline them, you can focus on the particular action they committed and why that was wrong. If they hit their playmates, ask them why they had to do that versus simply talking to them. If they cheated in a test, ask them what else they could have done to pass the test. If they made their siblings cry, then ask them if there is anything else they could have done to relate well with their siblings. When you zone in on the act and the other courses of action that are more appropriate for them, the child will understand that there is a better way of doing things that are not harmful to themselves or others. The child begins to see that other people are affected by their actions. In a way, you are teaching them the consequences of their actions.

If your child failed in school, try to probe what makes them have a difficult time. Is it the lesson itself? Is it the teacher? Are they distracted by their classmates? Do they have an eye problem that causes them not to see the things written on the blackboard? Are they finding the pace too fast? It is good to really go down to the details because this will tell you where to act on. If you simply let go of the failure and hope that things turn out better the next time, then the failure has lost its opportunities to teach us a lesson. You want the child to avoid that failure, and so they must learn from it. The way to learn is to go through the details of the incident and find ways to remedy the problem.

Finally, you have to lead the child into action. After being angry or sad and understanding what the issue really is, what can the child do at this point? You have to lead the child to solve their problems for themselves. When you give your opinion, then you lose the opportunity to make the child think for themselves. For example, if Raoul's problem is that his chosen friends don't want to have lunch with him for some unknown reason, then you can ask what Raoul can do. Perhaps he can look for other friends or focus on his studies first. Perhaps he can invite his friends over to the house, and Mom can cook for them. Do not settle with one course of action. If you can generate many possible courses of action, you allow the child the freedom to choose which one will best address their needs.

Later on, they will be thankful to you for teaching them this particular method of solving problems. When they can accept what they are feeling and generate different perspectives and courses of actions to remedy it, they will feel more empowered to bounce back and confront their failures head on. It is important that you validate their feelings and not brush them off as trivial. Children as they may be, their feelings are still real to them. Just patiently invite them to move from their feelings to thinking about what to do with their situation. Sometimes, there is really no course of action except just to let the matter slide. It happens. But that incident should leave them with some lesson that they can learn from.

Turn Negatives to Opportunity

One way you can turn the unfortunate event is really to help them see opportunities. Usually, failures and rejections are just sources of shame and insecurity. But children should be taught to embrace failures as teaching points they can actually convert into something productive. We have to lessen the stigma of failure. Yes, we don't like failures because they represent some form of deficiency in us. But we also don't want to dwell in failure because nothing can be achieved when we simply wallow in self-pity. You may invite your child to think of how to turn each failure into an opportunity.

For example, if they failed in a Math test, how could they turn that into an opportunity? Perhaps it's time they befriend a classmate who is good at Math and can help them with the lesson. Perhaps they can talk to their teacher so they can have extra exercises to work on at home. Perhaps they can buy more learning materials about Math to supplement the lesson. Whatever the problem is, there are a million ways to turn it into a strength. You need to tap into the child's creativity in reimagining a problem to be a challenge worth solving. This is important because failure is not regarded with fear and shame but as a point to become more creative in problem-solving. Children will not be afraid to try again and again because they will feel that failing is not a death sentence but an opportunity to learn.

Try, Try And Try Again

What is the best way to bounce back from a failure? Try again. Children will have to learn early on this valuable lesson of never giving up. This indefatigability is the antidote to depression. Instead of locking themselves in their rooms, people should face the challenge of failures and try and try again. They may not succeed in their next attempts. But as they encounter failure after failure, they should keep learning from it. At some point, they will be able to achieve what they want because the failures have guided them well. But they will not reach that level when they have given up the fight to try again. Cliché as it may seem, but the saying "It's not how many times you fall that matters; what matters is how many times you rise after each fall" is true.

Maybe you can even share your own stories of struggle. It is good when they feel that you are a relatable adult instead of all-powerful and perfect. Share to your child how you may have had difficulty in school before but was able to overcome it. Maybe you can tell them about your stories of difficulties with friends and how you managed that. Maybe you can share your experiences of being rejected and how you dealt with it. When they listen to your stories, they will feel inspired. By sharing your vulnerabilities, they can relate to their own limitations. If Daddy was poor in Math too and was able to pass in school, then I can also do well in school. If Mommy didn't have many friends before but had just one or two close ones, then perhaps I can also not feel very insecure about having just one friend. Your example will push them to also try and try and try again.

VIII

RECOVERING FROM TRAUMA

When we first brought Lily home, she was just clinging to me all the time. I thought that was her way of being affectionate. Maybe she was afraid of a new environment. And so I just let her hug me most of the time. Gradually, she was able to adjust to her new surroundings. She was 7. We got her through an agency that matched us with an institution in a faraway state. My husband and I really wanted a daughter, and so Lily was our answered prayer.

Through the next few days, I felt that Lily was particularly closer to me than her father. She would talk very warmly with me, discussing her day and her feelings openly with me. But when her father would try to reach out, she would suddenly keep quiet and bow her head down. It was frustrating for my husband who wanted to be a good father to her, but he respected her polite refusals. Maybe she just needs a more motherly presence.

But after several months, it was quite obvious that Lily did not really like being with my husband. Lily would just look at me during meal times, as though there was a wall between her and her father. When he would accidentally touch her hand when passing plates, she would immediately dart a look of fear and anger at Frank. He was so apologetic about the incident and said that he meant no harm.

Frank was quite distressed about the situation. He respected Lily so much but he just couldn't reach her. I love our daughter. I really want us to be a close family. I wanted Frank and Lily to have a great connection with each other so we could be more relaxed at home. But we both knew Lily's behavior was very much connected to her past.

Even before we adopted Lily, we knew that she was abused. We were told of her story the first day when we went to her institution a few years ago. We went to her orphanage and sought a meeting with the administrator. We were received well and ushered into a small office. Lily's records were taken from a file and the administrator was kind enough to let us read through her narrative. Frank and I were crying so hard after reading through her report. We couldn't believe that Lily underwent so many traumatic experiences in her former family. I couldn't even finish reading her file because I couldn't stomach what was written.

Lily was abused by her biological father some years ago. She was an only child and was often left at home with her father when her mother left them for another man. One night, her father came home drunk and forced her to have relations with him. The incident happened another time, and the little girl couldn't tell anybody about it. It was only through the report of neighbors who heard whimpering and crying in their house that the father was arrested. Social services got her out and took her to a facility specializing in caring for abused children. Her father was imprisoned while her mother was nowhere to be found. The institution had taken care of her well and processed her papers for adoption.

We were thinking that her aversion to Frank might have something to do with her trauma with men. We called up the institution and asked for some kind of help. They were kind enough to listen to us and pointed out that maybe Frank kind of looked like Lily's father. They both had bushy beards. Lily may have been triggered by that detail.

This was going to be very difficult for all of us, but more for Lily. Frank was willing to take it more slowly and be more understanding of Lily's situation. He even shaved his beard completely. We were very careful about touching Lily and we wanted to respect her personal space. After some time, Lily was able to warm up to Frank. She still doesn't want to be touched by men but she can now talk to him freely. I guess we are slowly healing as a family.

One of the more painful stories in adoption is taking care of children who have been physically and sexually abused by their former parents. Rape is an unthinkable, horrendous act, but to do it on your own children escapes all understanding. But sadly, it happens, especially if the parents are engaged in some form of drug addiction. The father loses his rationality and forces himself on his child. Whatever it is, these people deserve to be rehabilitated elsewhere, far from their children. We are grateful to all the people involved in the rescue of abused children.

But the damage done on them can be crippling for the rest of their lives.

Child abuse affects both boys and girls, with girls being the more usual targets. They cause significant damage to the child in terms of their physical, emotional, mental, and psychological state. The child's reaction and coping mechanisms are dependent on the age of the incidents, the availability of emotional resources, and the time from being physically removed from the perpetrator. The stress from the abuse can overwhelm the brain's capacity to deal with the situation. This may be manifested in poor coping mechanisms that impede the child to function well in their new environment.

Common Behavior of Abused Children

First, we have to understand the specific behaviors of children who are abused. Because the incident is so horrifying and traumatizing, these children may not be willing to tell their own stories of abuse. And perhaps it is not good to actually bring it up with them, as the retelling may trigger them to become more agitated and angry. But you have to be aware of certain behaviors they are exhibiting, which may be warning signs of deep-seated issues. These include:

Aversion to Touch and Physical Contact

In cases of sexual abuse, touch is one of the most sensitive triggers for children about the traumatic event. They may associate all forms of touch to the abuse, even when the perpetrator is gone or the circumstance is appropriate. Even just hugging or holding their hands can already trigger their memories of the abuse. You have to respect this and refrain from expressing your love in this physical sense. Later on, during the course of therapy, they may be able to get past this. But do not force them to be hugged or to hold their hands when they are not ready for it.

Inappropriate Displays of Affection

The abuse can affect the child in an extreme sense wherein they crave affection. Yes, the abuse is traumatizing for them. But the sexual awakening in them has started because of the incident. They do not know how to handle these inappropriate desires, so they will express them in others. For example, abused girls can be more comfortable with men or be completely adverse to them. They may engage in flirting behavior just to get attention. They are doing these unconsciously because the sexual character of the abuse leaves them craving for some form of attention.

Bursts of Anger

There may be times when they will just explode for a trivial reason. It may just be a small trigger, for example, a lost pair of shoes or an argument over curfew, but their reaction can be out of proportion. These explosions underlie a great deal of emotions that have not been processed over the years. Their traumatic experiences have been repressed in their minds and kept on lock because it is shameful for them to discuss them. But when something comes up, the deep well of emotions can be unleashed. The surge and swing of emotions can be so drastic because the experiences have been piled up for a long time. Perhaps, the environment in their former home was also filled with outbursts of anger and so they may think this is the normal way of expressing their emotions.

Defiance

These children may also show stubbornness or inflexibility when you lay down rules in the house. They want to be in control of the situation and get what they want all of the time. When you reason out with them, they will explode in anger. For some, they will try to follow your rules, but in a passive-aggressive manner. Outwardly, they will go through the motions of obeying you. But they may resent you all the while, dragging their feet when told to help out in the house or giving a lot of side comments. Again, these may be behaviors that helped them cope with their situation at home or things they picked up from their former families. It will take a lot of patience and understanding to help them.

Lack of Remorse or Guilt

When they violate house rules you have set, they may not show any remorse or guilt. In the school setting, they may be engaged in aggressive behavior towards other children. You may even be called up in school to make you aware of their actions. When asked if they are sorry, they can simply shrug it off or make an insincere apology. This blunting of moral affect is a way of coping with the traumatic incident. It was so intense that they just learned not to be affected by things. In the process, even their values are compromised.

They were wronged by their parents, and so they may feel it's alright to wrong others, as long as they can get away with it. This tough persona was what helped them survive their ordeal. Again, this would entail a lot of counseling to unpack.

School Problems

Abused children may have problems in academics. They are still in the process of developing their brain, and because of the incident, some parts may be stunted. Their emotional baggage can also distract them from focusing on school. Their IQs may be normal and even exceptional, but they will feel insecure and unsure of themselves because of the traumatic memories. This manifests as learning disabilities or poor performance in school. The solution is not to get them more academic tutors but to help them process what they are feeling because they can focus on learning later on.

Engaging in Risky Behavior

Because of their early exposure to sexual activities, abused children may often show higher tendencies to engage in similarly risky behaviors such as smoking, drinking, taking illicit drugs, or even engaging in sexual acts at a very young age. They may have been traumatized by the event, but it also increased their curiosity about what else they can do with their bodies. They want to push the limits of morality and this can have destructive consequences. You have to watch out for this, not simply by prohibiting their exposure to these activities, but more importantly, processing their issues and providing a safe space for them to grow.

Suicidal Tendencies

These children may also be more predisposed to depression and anxiety. With issues of insecurity, lack of self-worth, and shame, these children may be more prone to feeling depressed. When they are unable to cope with their situation anymore, some of them even entertain suicidal thoughts. You have to watch out for this and never disregard any mention of a suicidal attempt. Consult a professional so that the child can be helped immediately.

***

How can we help our children who may have been victims of abuse? It is difficult but it is not impossible. Certainly, it is rewarding to take care of these children. Do not shy away from the challenge of taking care of an adopted child who experienced physical abuse. They need the most help, and they rely on your strength and support to rebuild themselves from the trauma. It will need to take a lot of inner emotional resources from you, a lot of understanding from your partner, and a supportive atmosphere to rehabilitate a child who has experienced abuse.

Here are some useful advice in taking care of these children.

Seek Professional help

As I have continually mentioned in this chapter, you will need a professional therapist's services to guide your child. There is a special training needed to care for them and you might not be able to provide that care on your own. Some doctors may even prescribe medications to help your child ease some of her symptoms. The trauma event affects the biopsychosocial makeup of your child. So if there are biological effects, the medications can address them effectively. The psychosocial needs will need to be addressed through the therapies. It is important for you to undergo these therapies as a family to understand what your child is going through and how you can help her concretely. Adopting them may be the best remedy to their trauma and you would want some professional guidance to provide that support.

Be Caring But Be Firm

This is the difficult balance of parenting you must be able to maintain: the balance between being caring for your child and also being firm with the rules. On the one hand, you need to provide your child who has experienced abuse with all the love and support you can muster. You want to be understanding and accommodating with their needs, providing them with unconditional love. But you also don't want them to be destructive to themselves and others. You want them to unlearn some of the bad habits and coping mechanisms they picked up with their former families. And they will resist these changes. So you really have to find a way to balance caring and being firm.

You can practice your care by being available to them. Usually, these children are neglected and suffer from a lot of insecurities related to being wanted. If you are present to them physically and emotionally, then they will feel that they are also wanted and loved. You may be tired from a day's work but exert some effort to spend time with them and listen to their stories. They may not talk about the incident on your first days, but with enough assurances from you, they will open up to you eventually. Listen with empathy. Do not judge or react with revulsion, even if their story makes you cringe. In the very telling, they will feel some sense of relief and healing, as though finally, someone can listen to their story. You may not need to hug them if they are not yet ready. But simply being there for them will already help them heal.

When you practice your firmness on them, be very specific on house rules. Tell them exactly what you expect them to do or not to do and provide reasons why. For example, you may want to be firm against drinking and smoking in the house. Do not just say it is prohibited to do these things in the house. Tell them exactly why it is harmful and why you are not allowing it. If you tell them that they have to be at home by 6PM, be firm with your rules. Explain that you don't want them wandering off in some place you do not know or mingling with strangers. They have to be guided exactly what is appropriate and inappropriate behavior. Do not use physical punishment on them because this will trigger their trauma. You have to find creative means of instilling positive discipline. This may involve curtailing some playtime privileges or helping with the house chores longer. Let the children feel your love more than your dominance. Do not explain that these are the rules because you are the parent and they have to obey. When you explain the rationale to them, they will begin to understand and follow you more promptly. These children are in dire need of a sense of direction which you can provide.

The only way you can enforce these rules on the children is if you model them. If you say no smoking and drinking in the house, they must not see you smoking or drinking. If you say that they must pack their toys in the right places, make sure that you are also organized with your things. Remember that children imitate adults, and they will look to you for reference. They have previously learned from abusive parents, and so you can correct that by modeling values in the right way. Never create a rule which you yourself cannot abide in.

IX

DISCLOSING DETAILS

"Mom, my friend Bobby says I'm adopted. Is this true?"

This is perhaps one of the most difficult questions I have been asked by my adopted son Hans. We loved him the moment that we saw him in the orphanage. He was still a baby back then, given up by a teenage mom. We knew we wanted him immediately when he held on to my husband Raymond's finger the whole time we visited. He had big curious eyes, always attracted to bright lights and movement. It took around six months to finally take him home and hold his hands for as long as he liked.

Growing up, he was a very inquisitive boy. He always wanted to be hugged and held, and he would ask a lot of questions. "Mommy, what happens if the sun wants to sleep longer? Daddy, what is a rainbow made of? Why do dogs go 'bow wow' and cats go 'meow'?" He could be tiring but he certainly had a lot of energy we wanted to nurture. We tried to answer all of his questions as honestly as we could. But his questions never ran out.

And now, we were stuck with a question for which I knew the answer, but I was reluctant to tell. My husband and I knew we wanted to be as open as possible to Hans. We didn't want to keep things secret from him because we also wanted him to be open to us. But we were also afraid of how he would take it. Will he run away after hearing he was adopted? Will he hate us and look for his parents? I was so afraid this day would come. But Raymond just held my hand and told me, "Well, it's about time! No secrets, remember honey?"

And so we took Hans to our room. He could sense that something was up, maybe because I was stammering. But he kept his cool.

"Mom, my friend Bobby says I'm adopted. Is this true?"

"Well honey, we love you very much. You're the best boy we can ever ask for. Yes, you are adopted. Do you know what that means?"

"Not really."

"Well, it means that you came from a different womb, not from Mommy. We took you in from an orphanage. That is a place where other children who were left by their parents are, and we fell in love with you.

"Does that mean that I have a different Mommy and Daddy? So are you my Mommy and Daddy really?"

This boy asks very difficult questions. I looked to Raymond and asked him to help out.

"Well," Raymond started, "to be honest, we really don't know who your biological parents are. Your Mommy and I simply looked for the best baby in the orphanage and we found you. So we are still your Mommy and Daddy. You might not have come from us, but we love you just the same. Whether you are adopted or our biological child, it doesn't matter. We love you no matter what and nothing is going to change that."

There was a long and uncomfortable silence. Hans was trying to take it all in. He was a brave boy but I can sense he was trying to figure out what he just heard. I wanted to hug him now but I felt he needed his own space.

"Well I guess it's alright. Was I really the cutest baby in the orphanage?"

There were many other questions Hans had as he was growing up. But we never hid anything from him. Maybe he will go looking for his biological parents. When that time comes, we will support all of his decisions. What will never change is our love for each other.

Anna and Raymond's experience is a fear shared by most adoptive parents. The question of informing your child about his adoption status has parents divided. Some advocate being totally open to it from the very beginning. Others will keep the secret to the death, and the adoptee will only learn about their status during the parent's funeral. Others will wait for a more appropriate time, delaying until they can no longer deny. The choice of disclosure is a sensitive topic among adoptive parents.

It is important first to uncover all the feelings parents may have as they approach this sensitive topic. The recognition of feelings is important because it allows us to name that emotion that influences our decisions. There shouldn't be any judgment or denial of feelings because all of them are legitimate. Nobody can tell you that it is not right to be protective of your child because that is your right as a parent.

How do you feel about telling your child that he is adopted? The question asks about your feelings, so don't answer what your child is feeling or what your partner may be undergoing. It is your feeling that must be examined. Some parents feel afraid that their adoptive child will leave them after knowing they are adopted. They are hesitant to disclose because they fear that the child will go looking for the biological parent. It is good at this point to return to your original motivations for adopting a child. Did you feel some sort of emptiness in your marriage that you think the child can fill? Did you feel a surge of love that wanted to care for another human being? The fear can come in because knowing the truth may expose you to the possibility of losing that child. Are you afraid that the child may be angry with you for keeping the adoption issue a secret? Are you worried that they will take it against you if you didn't disclose it sooner?

All of these feelings are legitimate and real. I am not saying that your worries will not happen. Some children do look for their biological parents at some point. But a great majority still return to their adoptive parents. My point here is that our feelings may come from a position of fear instead of love. We fear for ourselves and our possible loss rather than sharing a painful truth with your child. It is way easier to keep things a secret and keep the illusion of a perfect family because you want to protect your loved ones. But love is not afraid. Our actions should be motivated more by love than our own fears. If we feel that the timing is not yet right and the child is not yet able to understand, then it may be a good decision to postpone disclosure. But if we simply operate from a fear of being left, then what we are experiencing is not love but dependence. When we choose to love by being honest, we risk being hurt. But we also risk being loved in return. And that is very much worth the pain of disclosing.

What will the information do for the child? Knowing that they are adopted may form a sense of insecurity in adopted children. So many questions will probably be running in their minds. Why were they adopted in the first place? Where are their biological parents? Did they love them less? Are they inadequate as persons and so they were given up for adoption? These are some of the painful consequences of telling the truth to your child.

But at the same time, knowing their adoption status can be very liberating for the child and for everyone. If they see that nothing about your love has changed from the time they knew the truth to the present, then being adopted will not be a real issue. Perhaps, they will love you more as parents because they will realize that you deliberately chose to love them instead of creating your own. There can be a deeper sense of gratitude and appreciation for the good you've done. And you don't need to keep any more secrets in the family. You can concentrate on growing maturely as a family in other areas when the adoption issue slips quietly into the background. You have to weigh all of these consequences and see if these will benefit your child more.

The timing is all important when you make any conversation about the adoption issue. Very young children may be too young to comprehend technical terms like 'biological' versus 'adoptive' parents. They probably wouldn't know the difference and the conversation may not be fruitful. On the other hand, when they are teenagers, these children will already be developing their own minds. They have their own opinions, own sets of friends, beliefs, and support systems. There can be a sense of betrayal when they feel you've kept things from them. The best age you can disclose is when the child is starting to form their independent reasoning skills. If they are able to ask you questions like Hans', then they are at a right age to know. They might not understand it fully the first time you disclose it. But trust that they are children who will understand in time.

I am a firm believer in this open disclosure because I really can't keep anything from Raoul. I told him he was adopted at age 7 and he took it well. He still has questions but I want him to feel that it is ok to talk about it in our house. I'd rather talk about it inside the home than he hears from his friends or strangers. I cannot control his thinking or his desire to look for his parents. That is beyond me. All I can do is really continue loving him. And I want to empower parents to operate out of love and not from fear. Here are some useful tips you can use when you have made the decision to disclose.

Use of Language

The way you explain it to your child is important. You will need to use terms which your child can understand in his age group. Do not use euphemisms like 'You came from the stork" because that will confuse your child more. Do not also use vague words like "You came from down there" because the child will not understand. You can also not use very technical words like "You were formed from the impregnation of an egg and a sperm" because it will simply add to the confusion. If you are clear with your language and appropriate for the child's language development, then the explanation is facilitated better.

Perhaps you need to explain to them what a parent is. You might try to distinguish between a biological parent and an adoptive parent. The biological parents are the ones who have conceived and given birth to the child. The adoptive parents are the ones who took the child into their home and raised them as their own. But after explaining this distinction, you can simply ask to be called 'parents' simply. It shouldn't be an issue whether you are the biological or adoptive parent. You are the child's parents. And that explanation should be sufficient for them. Again, you might need to practice how you will say things so that you don't get the child confused with the terms.

Sense of Normalcy

There shouldn't be a stigma with being adopted. After disclosing, there shouldn't be any changes in the way you deal with your child. It will seem awkward to start being overly loving and attentive to your child after disclosure. It feels more like a compensation on your part just to ease the tension away, which is not necessary. Just continue being the kind of parents you are to them as though nothing happened. They will appreciate this sense of normalcy because they will feel that the knowledge of being adopted has not changed the way they are loved. If you don't make adoption an issue, then it will not be an issue for the child.

You can control the settings at home but you may not be able to do so beyond it. Knowing that they are adopted can set these children up for discrimination and bullying in school or among friends. This is deplorable, but it really does happen. An innocent question from a friend like "Is it true that you are adopted?" can be a cause of hurt for the adopted child. They know they feel safe in the house, but the outside world may not be as sensitive.

In these instances, you have to teach your child to be secure about themselves. They have to get used to being asked this question because it really is part of who they are. They need not be overly defensive about it because they are still loved regardless of their status. They can simply reply, "Yes, I'm adopted. Is there a problem?" When the child is able to explain his status normally to other people, they will also feel that adoption is quite normal after all. The sense of security and calmness you deliver in disclosing to your child will transmit to their own security and calmness in explaining to others. They don't need to tell everybody they are adopted as some sort of advocacy drive. But they can respond well when they are asked. The more normal we feel about our child being adopted, then the more normal other people will feel when they encounter other adopted children.

Unwavering Support

When you can set the adoption issue aside, you can now concentrate on simply supporting the child in his or her endeavors. After all, they are children, and adoption is just one part of their identity and not the sole determinant of their personhood. The knowledge of being adopted should not hinder them from pursuing whatever it is that they want. If they want to paint and draw, provide them with the necessary materials to express themselves. If they want to excel in sports, cheer them on their games. If they want to pursue a particular career, assure them that they will have your support. The adoption issue is only one small part of an identity they are starting to form on their own. Let them focus on that identity-building with unwavering support.

***

Should there be a time when they feel that they want to find their biological parents, it can be a source of insecurity for adoptive parents. They may feel as if they are incomplete. That is why their child is looking for other parents. Again, this thinking operates on fear and not love. If you love your child and are confident in his love for you, you should trust him no matter what decision he makes. Like all other parents, we worry that our child will fail and commit mistakes. There is a legitimate fear of being left to ourselves in our old age, whether you have an adopted or a biological child. It is part of being a parent. But it is also our duty as parents to trust that we have raised our children well and can commit their own decisions and mistakes on their own. They can determine the life they want for themselves, as long as we are assured that we have loved them the best way we can.

X

CONCLUSION

I'm always happy to see Sarah leading Raoul by the hand as they walk in the street whenever we go to the grocery. She makes sure that Raoul is on the safer side of the road and prevents him from darting across the street. I can see Raoul clinging closely to Sarah's hand, trusting that his big sister will always protect him. When I see them walking on the street holding hands, I just want to capture that moment and hope it lasts forever. I do not see one biological daughter and one adopted son. I see my children leading each other by the hand.

As I end this book, I hope that I have empowered you in making this important decision to adopt. This must be one of the greatest things you will ever do for another human being, to take them in your home and shower them with the love they have not experienced. I think that more than what we can give our adopted children, they are giving more to us by their simple laughter and tears, their energy and tantrums, their unique gift of personhood. These lessons are culled from real people who have made that brave jump to save another human being through adoption. And they may not be perfect, but their experience is something we can learn and be inspired from.

I would like to end this book with some more insights that I couldn't classify in the other chapters. These are important values I think you should be considerate of whenever you feel challenged in dealing with adopted children. They are a joy to have, of course, but you will really encounter peculiar difficulties when you commit to raising them up well. It will take one adoptive parent to another adoptive parent to realize how unique our situation is. I am not saying that we are better parents than those who don't have adopted children. But I feel that we have a special mission which we need to take care of in our unique way.

First, don't forget that you are taking care of the child as a team. Most of the anecdotes I used are from mothers because they are the more vocal ones in sharing experiences. They are more hands-on in terms of rearing children. But I have seen husbands and fathers who are as invested in their children as their wife is. They may not like to be interviewed but I am sure that they love their adopted children equally. Do not leave your husband out of the picture. Assuming that you are a couple, you are raising them as parents and not as a parent only. When only one parent is involved and the other is half-hearted, the child can really sense this. They may be very close to you but very distant from the other. They may even be reminded of their past traumatic experiences because of the difference in parenting. I know that things will never be perfectly well for two people all the time in a marriage. You will have your ups and downs as a couple and as parents. But work together as a team. When one of you feels very down, support each other. When one feels doubt about how to raise your child, listen to each other. When one feels insecure that you are loving your child more than him, love each other more. Remember that love is multiplicative, not divisive. When you begin seeing parenting as the work of two people, you will begin to approach your child with more patience and compassion, with more firmness and determination that they get the best in the world. You won't get burned out as easily if you work together as a team rather than as individuals.

The work of siblings is also as important. If you have a mix of biological and adopted children, make sure everybody is on the same page. They are all children and there should be no hierarchy in terms of affection. Do not neglect any of them.

Indeed, you cannot treat them equally, but you can love them equally well. Adopted kids may have more needs than your other children, but do not forget that you have other children and have their own needs. Siblings should also be very supportive of each other. Rather than focus on the difference between biological and adopted, they should treat each other more normally as siblings. Fights are inevitable as children will be children. Let them have them but at the end of the day, make sure that there are mutual respect and love. Parents' work is greatly relieved when other siblings step up, help, and love each other.

Next, it is also important to work with the school in terms of managing your child. Adopted children don't need special attention. The more you declare that they should be given special treatment and priority, the more their status of being adopted becomes problematic for them. Ask simply for fair and equal treatment. If there are instances of bullying, you would want to know and confront the issue early. If there are any difficulties in academics, you would want to know to investigate where the problem lies. Some of these challenges in the school can be rooted in the child's traumatic past. But children also possess the unique capability of resiliency. They can bounce back from their past and conquer their own challenges given your support. You may not need to intervene yourself all of the time. But make sure that you establish open lines with the school and those that deal with your child on a daily basis.

You may also want to coordinate well with the institution or agency that handled your child. Adoptive parents feel that once they get their child, they may not have to hear from the institution anymore. But it is crucial that you understand where the child came from. As a parent, you would want to know everything about your son and daughter and their experiences before you. This is not to judge the caregivers or the biological parents. Pointing fingers will not solve anything for the child. It is constructive to establish a baseline in understanding the story of your child. From this, you will know what behaviors you can expect and how you can help your child concretely. It may not be healthy for you to establish contact with the biological parents because this may lead to many sensitive issues that may confuse or harm your child in the future. But you may just want to know what has happened and how you can all move forward.

Work closely also with the child's therapists and developmental pediatricians. These professionals will help you transition the child from their former families and institutions to your home. They have studied all about your child's potential problems and how to manage them, so trust that they know what they are doing. You might also need some form of professional help, especially when you may be lost or burnt out from taking care of your children. It is not shameful to ask for help. The stigma of consulting therapists actually delays the help and healing you could have been undergoing already. It is not a sign of weakness to ask for help but rather a strength you should build on.

It really takes a village to raise a child and an entire community to raise an adopted child. By showing you many people who may be involved in caring for your adopted child, I have also introduced your sources of strength and comfort. Your partner, your children, the teachers in school, the institution and agencies your children were previously placed, and therapists are all there to help your child become better. They will help you when you feel down and assure you that you are a good parent because you keep trying to become the best one for your kids.

Finally, I would like to invite you to chronicle your children's growth. I love taking pictures of my family in different stages. I have kept Raoul's picture in the orphanage, our first day in the house, his first toys, his first tantrum, his first haircut, his first birthday, and a million other firsts. On my cell phone, I have kept photographs of our family trips, our mealtimes, reunions, baptisms, special occasions, and ordinary days in our life as a family. It won't be long before your children become taller than you, so you better document everything that you can. You want to show them these precious memories. You will all be reminded not just of the specific events that have happened to you but also the consistent love you have for each other. It is really nice just to look back at how you have all grown as a family. And I think your children will appreciate these encapsulated memories and be grateful for all the love that they received.

If you are that type, I would also suggest that you make a diary to document your child's progress. Yes, pictures are worth a thousand words. But a diary can capture your innermost thoughts in a fuller way. It is good to jot down your learnings for the day, insights into parenting you may have come across, and anecdotes that you feel are worth remembering. The thought can quickly escape you, so typing them down in some permanent way will help you go back to the experiences and learn from them again and again. Like baby books, these diaries will help you remember your child's development. But it is also a cathartic way for you to express yourself. Let this diary be a witness and companion to your struggles and joys as a parent.

I salute you from the bottom of my heart for choosing to adopt. I feel that we have healed some of the world's pain whenever we multiply our love and open our homes to people who might not be biologically related to us but we consider as family. May your connectedness become stronger as you adopt all these lessons.

Review

As an independent author with a small marketing budget, reviews are my livelihood. If you enjoyed this book, I would really appreciate your honest feedback. I love hearing from my readers and I personally read every single review. This will also help me grow and share my knowledge with more people.

Thank you,

Nancy

9 798700 196888